IS-650.A: Building Partnerships with Tribal Governments

By

Fema

6/11/2010

IS-650: Building Partnerships with Tribal Governments

Lesson 1: Getting Started

Course Overview

Effective partnerships form and evolve because the individual partners have an understanding, appreciation, and respect for one another that is acquired through education and life experiences.

This course is designed to provide you with the basic knowledge to:

- Build effective partnerships with tribal governments.
- Work in concert with tribal governments to protect native people and property against all types of hazards.

Throughout this course tribal representatives speak to us about their history, their culture, their way of life, and what we need to know to develop good relationships with tribal communities.

These representatives provide insight into tribal communities that have endured great suffering and faced many challenges while remaining proud and committed to caring for one another, their land, and their traditions.

Several lessons are devoted to specific program challenges that you may encounter in working with tribal governments to provide financial and technical assistance through the Individual Assistance, Public Assistance, and Hazard Mitigation Programs.

For example, the course addresses how to let native people who live in remote areas and are not served by traditional print and mass media know about how and where to apply for disaster assistance.

The program challenges presented in the course reflect actual experiences of native people and FEMA representatives working together before, during, and after disasters to deliver assistance in Indian Country.

Throughout the course, you will be able check your knowledge by answering general questions about the material and by applying what you have learned to a disaster scenario. After completing all eight lessons, you can take the final examination online. An Independent Study Program Certificate of Achievement will be issued if you score at least 75 percent on this examination.

Introduction

In this lesson, you will learn:

- Basic facts about Native Americans.
- Challenges faced by Federal workers and tribal members when working together.

Given a flood-disaster scenario, you will predict issues that disaster workers and tribes may face in relating to one another.

Partnering Challenges

Like other U.S. citizens and local governments, American Indians and tribal governments may be eligible for Federal disaster assistance and other programs that benefit individuals and their communities.

Tribal communities present a special challenge to government workers. For example:

- Sometimes the State and local emergency management network overlooks tribal governments.
- Tribal cultures and traditions may conflict with work expectations and procedures.
- Indian communities often mistrust representatives of the Federal Government.

Disaster Worker Challenges

Del Brewer, Former FEMA Employee

I'm amazed when FEMA people say we should deal with tribes the same way as any other applicants for assistance. Tribes are sovereign governments that want to deal directly with the Federal Government.

Every tribe is different, the leadership is different, the protocol for contacting them is different. I find someone who knows about that tribe to tell me how to approach the leadership.

Joan Rave, FEMA Employee

In 1992, a flood recovery operation in Arizona forced us to flex the Stafford Act to its limit in order to achieve the Congressional mandate of getting assistance to all eligible applicants. The Major Disaster area included 11 federally recognized Indian tribes-among them the Navajo (the largest landed tribe in the U.S.), the Hopi (who have lived on ancient mesas for hundreds of years), Havasupai (their Reservation is at the bottom of the Grand Canyon), and others.

The FEMA Emergency Response Team, most of us from the Seattle area and few of us with tribal experience, set out to deliver assistance in communities that existed before Columbus landed; where English is a second language; and where Federal agents and other non-tribal governments are viewed with suspicion and considered to be the cause of cultural alienation and political disenfranchisement.

Tribal Considerations

Many tribes are new to emergency management and disaster assistance. Some things you should consider are:

- Tribal communities traditionally care for their own people in disasters.
- Tribal leaders may not know how to ask for Federal disaster assistance.
- Tribal people may see FEMA's role as interference with tribal culture.
- Tribal people often do not distinguish among government agencies.

Above all, remember that good relations depend on respect for tribal leadership structures and decisionmaking processes.

Tribal viewpoints reflect a range of experience with emergency management and with FEMA.

Julie Bator, elected official, Alaska Native Village of Tazlina

I think FEMA is a myth to people in our area. I think FEMA has been seen as assisting hurricane victims in Florida, flood victims in North Dakota. And it seems like our community is too small, and the reaction we've gotten from other Federal agencies has been so minimal to our needs and wants that we have not ever expected FEMA to pay attention to us.

Unless it was a drastic emergency, they wouldn't want your interference because people would come from neighboring villages, as they always do, to support our families and other people within our clan, and take care of our own. And we pride ourselves in being able to do that.

Tim Sanders, Emergency Manager, Gila River Indian Community

It would be important to find out who the tribal chairperson or the president or the governor is. It's important to communicate on that government-to-government level.

Tribal officials, elders in particular, will really want to explain what their point is, and they may take a little while to do that. And it's important that you respect that and not try to rush that conversation along, not try to get to the endpoint. There have been instances in working with FEMA where, maybe in preliminary damage assessments and things like that, FEMA is used to working with counties and State governments that are used to working quickly and getting that information to FEMA. It may not always happen that quickly at the tribal government level.

Lesson 2: Historical & Legal Perspectives

Historical Timeline

There have been radical shifts in policy toward Indian nations that negatively impacted the cultures, identities, and ancestral lands of these great nations.

The historical timeline for these major changes falls within seven periods:

- Pre-European Period (Prior to 1492)
- Colonial Period (1492-1828)
- Removal and Relocation Period (1828-1871)
- Allotment and Attempted Assimilation Period (1871-1928)
- Reorganization Period (1928-1945)
- Termination and Relocation Period (1945-1965)
- Self-Determination Period (1965-Present)

This lesson is designed to help you learn about what occurred in each of these periods and its effect on Native Americans.

Pre-European Period (Prior to 1492)

What was it like in the America that greeted the first Europeans? You may be surprised to learn it was far from a wilderness with uncivilized inhabitants.

Come with me as we travel back to that period and see what it was really like.

The population was in the millions and may have matched the population numbers for Western Europe. These numbers would be reduced drastically as a result of war and the diseases introduced by the new settlers: diseases like smallpox, typhus, and influenza.

The native's diet was varied and plentiful. Most tribes combined aspects of hunting, gathering, and the cultivation of maize and other food supplies. Every tomato in Italy, every potato in Ireland, and every hot pepper in Thailand came from this hemisphere. Corn, or maize as it is known, spread throughout the earth as the Indians cultivated many varieties for different growing conditions. The use of Indian crops throughout the world dramatically reduced hunger and led to a population boom in the Old World. Indians produced bumper crops of elk, deer, and bison by cultivating the environment.

They used fire for two reasons: to keep down underbrush and create open, grassy spaces required for the game to populate. The first white settlers in Ohio found forests as open as English parks in which they could drive carriages through the woods. The use of fire shaped the plains that created the environment for vast buffalo farms.

Indian life was essentially clan-orientated and communal, with children allowed more freedom and tolerance than European children. While some clans were nomadic, many others lived in settlements. For example, in what is now the southwest United States, the Anasazi, ancestors of the modern Hopi Indians, built stone and adobe pueblos. These unique and apartment-like structures were often built along cliff faces. The most famous, the "cliff palace" of Mesa Verde, Colorado, had over 200 rooms.

Indian society was closely tied to the land and the rhythms and spirit of nature. Indians believe that if you take care of Mother Nature she will take care of you. This was in direct conflict with the Europeans, who considered land and nature a commodity to be owned and used for their individual purposes. This difference would later be the source of much of the conflict that occurred between the native and European cultures.

As a way of preserving their culture some North American tribes developed a type of hieroglyphics, but mostly they depended on oral communications. Even today, history and values are handed down from generation to generation through the recounting of tales and dreams.

Tribes routinely interacted with one another through trade and extensive formal relations, quite an accomplishment considering there were hundreds of different languages spoken.

The ideals of democracy and equality are ideals that were part of the Indian way of life. Both men and women had a say in the tribe's decisions. The colonists had no experience with democracy as they had lived under the rule of monarchies and generally referred to the native village leaders as kings.

Rather than a backward nation of indigent people, the Europeans found themselves in a populous new world more sophisticated than what they had left behind.

Colonial Period (1492-1828)

The movement to North America grew from a trickle of a few hundred European colonists to a flood of millions of newcomers. Why did they leave Europe in mass? For most people, it was to:

- Escape political oppression of the ruling parties.
- Find freedom to practice their religion.
- Avoid economic difficulties sweeping England.

Colonial Period (1492-1828): Early Colonists

The settlers acquired Indian lands through the doctrine of discovery (simply locating land and laying claim to it), transfer from the English crown, and treaties with the Indians.

Treaties are documents between two independent sovereignties to negotiate borders, provide access to resources, and settle land and military disputes.

The colonists settled mostly on the east coast because the English government had forbidden encroachment of the colonists west of the Appalachians. This policy was intended to maintain peace with the Indian tribes and discourage any alliance between them and France.

Colonial Period (1492-1828): Post-Revolutionary War

Following the Revolutionary War, the United States continued the treatymaking with the tribes started by the Spanish and British. These treaties or agreements, negotiated on a government-to-government pattern, sought to establish peace and territorial boundaries and to regulate trade and extradition of criminals.

The 1778 Treaty With the Delaware Indians was the first between the United States and an Indian tribe.

TREATY WITH THE DELAWARES 1778

Sept. 17 1778, 7 Stat., 13. [3]

Articles of agreement and confederation, made and entered into by Andrew and Thomas Lewis, Esquires, Commissioners for, and in Behalf of the United States of North-America of the one Part, and Capt. White Eyes, Capt. John Kill Buck, Junior, and Capt. Pipe, Deputies and Chief Men of the Delaware Nation of the other Part.

ARTICLE I. That all offences or acts of hostilities by one, or either of the contracting parties against the other, be mutually forgiven, and buried in the depth of oblivion, never more to be had in remembrance.

ARTICLE II. That a perpetual peace and friendship shall from henceforth take place, and subsist between the contracting parties aforesaid, through all succeeding generations: and if either of the parties are engaged in a just and necessary war with any other nation or nations, that then each shall assist the other in due proportion to their abilities, till their enemies are brought to reasonable terms of accommodation: and that if either of them shall discover any hostile designs forming against the other, they shall give the earliest notice thereof, that timeous measures may be taken to prevent their ill effect.

ARTICLE III. And whereas the United States are engaged in a just and necessary war, in defence and support of life, liberty and independence, against the King of England and his adherents, and as said King is yet possessed of several posts and forts on the lakes and other places, the reduction of which is of great importance to the peace and security of the contracting parties, and as the most practicable way for the troops of the United States to some of the posts and forts is by passing through the country of the Delaware nation, the aforesaid deputies, on behalf of themselves and their nation, do hereby stipulate and agree to give a free passage through their country to the troops aforesaid, and the same to conduct by the nearest and best ways to the posts, forts or towns of the enemies of the United States, affording to said troops such supplies of corn, meat, horses, or whatever may be in their power for the accommodation of such troops, on the commanding officer's, &c. paying, or engageing to pay, the full value of whatever they can supply them with. And the said deputies, on the behalf of their nation, engage to join the troops of the United States aforesaid, with such a number of their best and most expert warriors as they can spare, consistent with their own safety, and act in concert with them; and for the better security of the old men, women and children of the aforesaid nation, whilst their warriors are engaged against the common enemy, it is agreed on the part of the United States, that a fort of sufficient strength and capacity be built at the expense of the said States, with such assistance as it may be in the power of the said Delaware Nation to give, in the most convenient place, and advantageous situation, as shall be agreed on by the commanding officer of the troops aforesaid, with the advice and concurrence of the deputies of the aforesaid Delaware Nation, which fort shall be garrisoned by such a number of the troops of the United States, as the commanding officer can spare for the present, and hereafter by such numbers, as the wise men of the United States in council, shall think most conducive to the common good.

Colonial Period (1492-1828): Key Case Law - Marshall Trilogy

In 1823, Chief Justice John Marshall wrote the first of three cases of key Federal Indian law that affirmed tribal sovereignty and established doctrine of Federal trust responsibility. These laws are known as the Marshall Trilogy and are the foundation for current judicial decisions involving the powers of tribes. Summaries of these cases follow.

Johnson v. M'Intosh, 21 U.S. (8 Wheat) 543 (1823)
This case involved competing claims to the same lands acquired from the same Indian tribe by different means. The court ruled that Indian nations could only convey ownership to the United States and not individuals. This approach restrained encroachment not authorized by the United States into Indian territories and confirmed Federal control of Indian affairs.

Cherokee Nation v. Georgia, 30 U.S. (5 Pet.) 1 (1831)
The Cherokee Nation challenged the legality of the State of Georgia to oust the Cherokee Nation

from its lands in spite of its treaty with the United States. Judge Marshall ruled that the Cherokee Tribe is a "domestic dependent nation" with the relation of the tribe to the Federal Government like that of "ward to guardian." Therefore, the State could not interfere with the Cherokee Nation.

Worcester v. Georgia, 31 U.S. (6 Pet.) 515 (1832)
Missionaries to the Cherokee Nation appealed their conviction in Georgian courts for not having received a license from the Governor of Georgia to enter Cherokee country. Judge Marshall ruled the conviction by the State was void because the tribe was a distinct community over which the laws of the State have no force.

Colonial Period (1492-1828): Bureau of Indian Affairs

The Bureau of Indian Affairs was created to manage the affairs of the tribes in fulfillment of the Federal Government's self-determined role as having power over Indian affairs. The mission has changed dramatically over time from the direct provider of services to that of technical specialist working with tribal managers in protecting and managing trust resources.

Removal and Relocation Period (1828-1871)

As the U.S. population continued to grow and the demand for land on the east coast increased, the U.S. Government forced eastern tribes to move west.

In 1835, nearly all of the Cherokee Nation—some 17,000 people—were forced to leave their ancestral lands, homes, and possessions at gunpoint and forced to march from northern Georgia to present-day Oklahoma. The Trail of Tears, as it is known, killed 4,000 Cherokee.

Removal and Relocation Period (1828-1871): Moving Tribes West

Nearly all the eastern tribes were moved from fertile soil to the semiarid center of the country—known at the time as the Great American Desert. Consequently, today there are very few tribes located on the east coast.

The removal policy gave way in the 1850s to an official policy of confining Indians to reservations rather than relocating them beyond the rapidly expanding frontier.

Removal and Relocation Period (1828-1871): Treaties Ceding Lands

Throughout this period, hundreds of treaties were made. Many of them were made with tribes in the Northern Plains for their lands, thus restricting reservation boundaries even further.

Some of these treaties contained provisions for the tribes to retain hunting, fishing, and gathering rights on the ceded lands. These treaty rights are still valid and must be considered when carrying out the provisions of programs that could impair these rights.

Removal and Relocation Period (1828-1871): Violating Treaties

Unfortunately, some of the treaties were never ratified, and some were put in place through bribery or by only a small part of the signatory tribes. Additionally, the Federal Government failed to fulfill the terms of many treaties, and was sometimes unable or unwilling to prevent States, or white people, from violating treaty rights of Indians.

By 1871, treatymaking came to an end. The treaties were replaced with agreements that the executive branch negotiated and the Congress enacted into law. The move was mostly symbolic and ushered in the beginning of the next era.

Allotment and Attempted Assimilation Period (1871-1928)

During this period:

- More Indian lands were taken for settlement by the United States.
- Federal law expanded into internal tribal affairs.
- Widespread use of boarding schools for Indian children developed.
- Reserved tribal lands were allotted to individual Indian ownership.

Allotment and Attempted Assimilation Period (1871-1928): General Allotment Act

The General Allotment Act (Dawes Act) sought to break up tribes by breaking up the ownership of the land and assimilating them into the Nation. Specifically, the act:

- Enabled the President to allot small parcels of tribal lands to individual Indians.
- Authorized the Federal Government to hold land in trust for 25 years or more to prevent transfer of the land.
- Authorized the United States to sell lands left after allotment.
- Subjected allottees to State civil and criminal jurisdiction.
- Extended U.S. citizenship to allottees.

Allotment and Attempted Assimilation Period (1871-1928): "Surplus" Land

Under the original act, heads of household and minors received 160 and 40 acres, respectively. This was soon changed to reduce the amount of acreage.

Of the 138 million acres in Indian or tribal lands in 1887, only 48 million acres remained by 1934. Most of the loss resulted from what was called **surplus land**—i.e., whatever land remained after allotments were made to Indian households of their own lands. Some of the surplus lands were sold and payments made to the tribes while others were simply opened for homesteading.

Allotment and Attempted Assimilation Period (1871-1928): Removing Children From Their Families

Federal Indian policy called for the removal of children from their homes and, in many cases, enrollment in Government-run boarding schools far away from their families.

Allotment and Attempted Assimilation Period (1871-1928): Destroying Tribal Traditions

Julie Bator, elected official, Alaska Native Village of Tazlina

We have 227 different ways to say "fish" and it's very descriptive, and it's going to be gone. Missionaries who came into our area in the late 1800s or early 1900s shipped off the young people into European or American schools.

My grandfather was one of those people.

They taught them it was not right to speak Athabaskan, and just slapped their hands and hit them for speaking Athabaskan in their dorms. They were physically punished for continuing that part of their culture.

Consequently, my father does not know the language.

Allotment and Attempted Assimilation Period (1871-1928): Granting U.S. Citizenship to Indians

In 1924, Congress granted Indians U.S. citizenship for the first time because of the services Indian soldiers performed during World War I and due also to lobbying efforts on behalf of Indians.

The Allotment and Attempted Assimilation Period came to a close as a result of a Government-requested study (the Merriam Report) that deemed the policies of this period a failure.

Reorganization Period (1928-1945)

This short but progressive period ended allotments and began restoring Indian lands. The Federal Government created programs and projects for health facilities, irrigation works, roads, homes, and schools to help restore Indian economic and cultural life.

Reorganization Period (1928-1945): Indian Reorganization Act

The Indian Reorganization Act (IRA), sometimes called the Indian New Deal, was the centerpiece of this era.

Instead of forcing Indian people to forsake their traditions for new lives on farms or in cities, the IRA recognized their right to exist as a separate culture.

The act included the establishment of chartered tribal governments with constitutions and bylaws based on a template of the Federal Government. This structure is very different from the traditional government structure of the tribes.

This period was the first time in American Indian history that tribal councils were formally recognized.

Termination and Relocation Period (1945-1965)

Termination basically ended what the Government previously endorsed:

- Trust relationships between Federal and tribal governments.
- Self-government of the tribes.

Termination and Relocation Period (1945-1965): Termination Policies and Results

More than 100 tribes were terminated during this period. The Federal Government simply no longer recognized them as Indian nations and ended Federal supervision and control over Indians.

The tribes lost their governmental authority and State criminal laws were imposed on many tribes. Additionally, millions of acres of valuable natural resource land were taken through tax forfeiture sales.

Termination and Relocation Period (1945-1965): Relocation Program

The Bureau of Indian Affairs started a relocation program that granted money to Indians to move to selected sites to find work—yet another attempt to absorb Indians into mainstream society and eliminate distinct cultures. This program was somewhat successful: 40% of the Indian population still resides in cities.

Self-Determination Period (1965-Present)

The abuses of the Termination and Relocation Period led to reforms. The Federal Government expanded the powers of tribal self-government and restored the recognition of tribes.

In a special message to Congress, President Lyndon B. Johnson stated his principles for tribal relations, which those who have followed him continue to support:

"The greatest hope for Indian progress lies in the emergence of Indian leadership and initiative in solving Indian problems. And we must assure the Indian people that it is our desire and intention that the special relationship between the Indian and his government grow and flourish. For the first among us must not be the last."

Self-Determination Period (1965-Present): Legislation

Important legislation includes the following:

- **Indian Civil Rights Act**: Establishes civil rights for all people under tribal government jurisdiction and authorizes the Federal Government to enforce these rights.
- **Indian Self-Determination and Education Assistance Act**: Recognizes the Federal trust responsibility and directs the Bureau of Indian Affairs and Indian Health Services to contract with the tribes for programs that these agencies administer such as education, health, and human services.
- **American Indian Religious Freedom Act**: Preserves the rights of American Indians to practice traditional religious beliefs.
- **Native American Graves Protection and Repatriation Act**: Requires notification and return of human remains and culture items to the tribes. Also regulates the excavation of land where Indian remains or property are located.

Self-Determination Period (1965-Present): FEMA Tribal Policy

Federal agencies have acknowledged their support for the independence and government-to-government relationships with the tribes through policy statements and removal of barriers to participation in national programs.

FEMA's tribal policy became effective in 1998.

FEMA is revising its tribal policy in 2010 to further define and emphasize the need for improved consultation and coordination between FEMA and tribal governments.

Excerpt from FEMA Tribal Policy

In recognition of the trust responsibility, the Federal Emergency Management Agency will evaluate to the extent possible the impact of policies, programs, and activities on Tribal trust resources and assure that it considers the rights and concerns of Tribal governments in its decisionmaking.

The Federal Emergency Management Agency will identify and take appropriate steps to the extent practicable to eliminate or diminish procedural impediments to working directly and effectively with Tribal governments.

The Federal Emergency Management Agency recognizes that there may be legal, procedural, organizational, or other impediments that affect its working relationships with Tribes. To the extent practicable and permitted by law, the Federal Emergency Management Agency will apply the requirements of Executive Order 12875, "Enhancing the Intergovernmental Partnership," and Executive Order 12866, "Regulatory Planning and Review," to design solutions and tailor Agency programs to address specific or unique needs of Tribal governments.

The Federal Emergency Management Agency will work in partnership with other Federal departments and agencies to the extent practicable to enlist their support of cooperative efforts to further the goals of this policy.

The Federal Emergency Management Agency recognizes the importance of interagency communication, coordination, and cooperation to pursue and implement its Tribal policy and to fulfill the Agency's commitment to work with Tribal governments in a government-to-government relationship.

The Federal Emergency Management Agency will encourage cooperation and partnership between and among Federal, Tribal, State, and local governments to resolve issues of mutual concern related to emergency management.

Effective emergency management requires the cooperation, partnership, and mutual consideration of neighboring governments, whether those governments are neighboring Tribal, State, or local governments. Accordingly, the Federal Emergency Management Agency will encourage pursuing partnerships in the interest of emergency management. The Agency's support is not intended to lend Federal support to any one party to the jeopardy of the interests of another. In the field of emergency management, problems are often shared and the principle of partnership between equals and neighbors often serves the best interests of both.

The Federal Emergency Management Agency acknowledges as precedents the policy commitments and decisions of the executive, legislative, and judicial branches of the United States Government.

The Federal Emergency Management Agency's policy for government-to-government relations with American Indian and Alaska Native Tribal governments reinforces and incorporates the commitments contained in various Presidential policies emphasizing that such a government-to-government relationship be pursued. The Agency's policy also recognizes the 1988 U.S. House of Representatives Concurrent Resolution #331, which declares the policy "To acknowledge the contribution of the Iroquois Confederacy of Nations... and to reaffirm the continuing government-to-government relationship between Indian tribes and the United States established in the Constitution." Further, this policy acknowledges the importance and precedence of treaties, court decisions, statutes, executive orders, and regulations regarding Tribal policy without extensive citations.

The Federal Emergency Management Agency will use its best efforts to institutionalize this policy within the fundamental tenets of the Agency's mission.

The Federal Emergency Management Agency will fully and effectively incorporate to the extent practicable all of the principles of this policy into the daily activities and operations of Agency employees. This policy is designed to reflect an ongoing and long-term planning and management effort.

Resources

- American Indian and Alaska Native Data and Links [http://factfinder.census.gov/home/aian/index.html]
- An Outline of American History [http://iipdigital.usembassy.gov/st/english/publication/2011/04/20110428150452su0.6368306.html]
- Bureau of Indian Affairs Frequently Asked Questions [http://www.bia.gov/FAQs/index.htm]
- Indian Law: An Overview [http://www.law.cornell.edu/topics/indian.html]
- Working Effectively with Federally-Recognized Indian Tribes. Environmental Protection Agency. Call for a copy: (202) 260-2516.
- An Introduction to Indian Nations in the United States. National Congress of American Indians. Call for a copy: (202) 466-7767. There is a charge for the booklet.

Lesson 3: Tribal Relations - Overview

Overview of Tribal Cultures

Narrator: Tribal people are bound together by shared traditions and values.

Julie Bator, Elected Official, Alaska Native Village of Tazlina: "I think we have the ability to overcome, adapt, and survive. And it's been demonstrated on every level for 4,000 years."

Narrator: Each tribe is different, with a unique history and culture.

Tim Sanders, Emergency Manager, Gila River Indian Community: "The worst thing to do would be to go in there with preconceived notions of what Indian people are."

Narrator: Stereotypes of Native Americans interfere with positive relations. There are even times when non-natives unintentionally insult Native Americans. For example . . .

Julie Bator: "I think assuming that all Alaskan Indians are alcoholics, that we all have limited educations and limited thinking capacities. It's really ignorant to assume ignorance."

Bernice Lalo, Elected Official, Western Shoshone: "One of the things we need to know about Indian life is that we have a history, and we have songs, we have dances, we have fine arts, we have literature, we have scientists, we have botanists, we have medical people."

Lawrence Lucero, Elected Official, Isleta Pueblo: "We do expect you to be sensitive and respectful for who we are as a people, and that you recognize the fact that we're a sovereign nation with its own form of government, and that you recognize the fact that we are a unique people in our own ways."

Narrator: Positive relationships begin with understanding. This lesson is designed to help you expand your understanding of tribal cultures.

Addressing Native Americans

If asked, tribal people will explain how they want to be addressed. Most prefer use of a specific tribal name.

Bernice Lalo, Elected Official, Western Shoshone

We were termed as "Indians." And I've never been an Indian in all of my life. I don't come from east India; I don't speak their language. However, I do speak Shoshone and we have a Shoshone nation, and those are—tribal people, we're indigenous from the land.

And I can't speak for other people, but I—if you were to describe me, I would be a Western Shoshone. Because I am a citizen of my own nation.

Julie Bator, Elected Official, Alaska Native Village of Tazlina

I guess the politically correct term is Alaska Native Indians. And one thing I would want people to know is that Alaskans, Alaskan Indians are not Eskimos. And that is something that if you were to learn about cultural sensitivity, it would be an important point for you to open a door.

If you wanted to continue your conversation with someone in our area and you called them an Eskimo, you would be sent out the door. And that would be the end of the conversation.

Lawrence Lucero, Elected Official, Isleta Pueblo

First of all, people need to recognize that we are first of all Pueblo and not just Indians. We also like to be recognized as Native American, and we're specifically Pueblo Indian. And that only pertains to our tribe, which is Pueblo.

So the preferred term is Native American or Pueblo Indian and not just Indian.

Family and Elders

The family holds a central place in all tribal cultures.

- Tribal families treat distant clan members as close relatives.
- Family needs outweigh other concerns and commitments.

Tribal communities show great respect for the wisdom of their elders by:

- Addressing them first in group settings.
- Consulting them about how to proceed.

Younger tribal members interpret as needed for elders with limited English.

Bernice Lalo, Elected Official, Western Shoshone

I have three brothers and three sisters, and I'm the fifth one down the road, and I have a younger sister. We were charged with getting water from the stream, by dippers, and filling up a great wooden barrel in our kitchen.

As we grew a little bit older and could handle machinery and could handle horses or work horses, we were given responsibility according to our age group.

My father said that we could do whatever we wanted to do or could do or could challenge, as long as we were waiting for whatever came afterwards, either the praise or the licks, as he would call it.

Julie Bator, Elected Official, Alaska Native Village of Tazlina

We take on the clan of our mothers, our grandmothers. Material goods are passed down, hunting territories are passed down through our mothers' line.

We respect our elders, which is something I'm really proud of and something I try to instill in my children, that they are valuable resources and the reason that we are still alive.

Addressing Native Americans

Tribal people carefully consider responses when answering questions and making decisions. Therefore, when working with tribal people, plan to double or triple the amount of time you would ordinarily expect to spend.

Also keep in mind that:

- A rushed and impersonal manner may shut off conversation.
- Information often is shared by telling a story.
- Tribal people consider it an insult to provide information you may already know; as a result, they can appear reluctant to answer a question or volunteer information.

Tim Sanders, Emergency Manager, Gila River Indian Community

Indians will typically approach things in a very deliberate manner. You've heard that old cliché about ask someone for the time, they'll tell you how to build a clock? A lot of times that will happen when you're speaking with tribal officials, elders in particular. And it's important that you respect that and not try to rush that conversation along, not try to get to the endpoint.

Julie Bator, Elected Official, Alaska Native Village of Tazlina

You might have to listen for a few minutes before you get your answer, and it might seem a story that doesn't relate to what you're talking about, but if they want you to think about things and come to your own conclusion, then it's part of our way not to tell you what to do. It's not right to tell another what to do.

Our elders aren't comfortable speaking to non-natives, a lot times you won't get the stories from them, and consequently they appear not to know what they're talking about or doing. And just because they're quieter or don't know how to say things in the English way doesn't mean that they don't have the knowledge or that they don't deserve your respect.

Hospitality

Most tribal cultures value hospitality, and may expect visitors to share food and drink.

Tim Sanders, Emergency Manager, Gila River Indian Community

They will really welcome you into their family, into their homes, try their best to make you feel at home.

Julie Bator, Elected Official, Alaska Native Village of Tazlina

They're going to be glad to see you, and they're going to ask you to come in, and they're going to try to feed you for about 2 hours. You need to respect that and eat it, at least a little of it. Drink some tea and have some hardtack or some cake or something. And they're going to try to keep you there. If you eat, you get your facts, and you can leave. But it's disrespectful to not—they consider it a trade. So you're going to be made to sit down.

Native Languages

In the United States, there are about 600 distinct tribal languages belonging to more than 10 language families. The ability to speak one's language is highly prized.

Bernice Lalo, Elected Official, Western Shoshone

We spoke English, we spoke Shoshone at the same time we learned to tie our shoes, and it was no different except finding the difference in who would answer you if you spoke Shoshone or English.

I've developed grants for the tax structure for my tribe, a library for my tribe, an environmental camp for young people, Shoshone native language for youth.

Lawrence Lucero, Elected Official, Isleta Pueblo

Isleta is only one of 19 Pueblos. All other Pueblos speak a different dialect; the dialect that Isleta Pueblos speak with is the Tiwa language.

The reason I bring up Tiwa is that's our first language, at least it was and it has been for many of our youth that are growing up. And this dialect is not written; it's learned through oral teaching and learning.

Worship

Religious traditions endure among tribal people. Expressions of spiritual life include:

- Dancing, singing, and chanting.
- Showing reverence by actions such as drinking water, burning sweet grass, taking a sweat bath, or fasting.
- Gathering for ceremonies in certain locations at specific times.
- Treating burial grounds and other traditional sites as sacred.

The circle carries special meaning for tribal people.

Why Indians Use the Circle

"You have noticed that everything an Indian does is in a circle, and that is because the Power of the World always works in circles, and everything tries to be round. In the old days when we were a strong and happy people, all our power came to us from the sacred hoop of the nation, and so long as the hoop was unbroken, the people flourished. The flowering tree was the living center of the hoop, and the circle of the four quarters nourished it. The east gave peace and light, the south gave warmth, the west gave rain, and the north with its cold and mighty wind gave strength and endurance. This knowledge came to us from the outer world with our religion. Everything the Power of the World does is done in a circle. The sky is round, and I have heard that the earth is round like a ball, and so are all the stars. The wind, in its greatest power, whirls. Birds make their nests in circles, for theirs is the same religion as ours. The sun comes forth and goes down again in a circle. The moon does the same, and both are round.

Even the seasons form a great circle in their changing, and always come back again to where they were. The life of a man is a circle from childhood to childhood, and so it is in everything where power moves. Our tepees were round like the nests of birds, and these were always set in a circle, the Nation's hoop, a nest of many nests, where the Great Spirit meant for us to hatch our children."

-Black Elk, Oglala Sioux Holy Man, 1863-1950

Relationship to Land

Traditionally, tribal people have not viewed land as the property of human beings. Because of these beliefs:

- Tribal members often share use of the land.
- Land is considered sacred.

Resources

- Learning about American Indian Culture Pocket-Sized Guide Describes Tribal Sovereignty, Myths & Facts, and More [http://download.ncadi.samhsa.gov/ken/pdf/SMA08-4354/CultureCard_AI-AN.pdf]
- National Museum of the American Indian [http://www.nmai.si.edu]
- Navaho Codetalkers [http://www.lapahie.com/NavajoCodeTalker.cfm]

Lesson 4: Tribal Relations - Initial Response

Providing Federal Disaster Assistance

The Stafford Act provides the authority for FEMA's role in managing Federal disaster assistance. This role includes:

- Helping assess the damage after a disaster.
- Evaluating a Governor's request for a Presidential declaration.
- Advising the President concerning recommendations for declarations.
- Working with the State and local governments in a joint partnership to implement the various assistance programs.
- Coordinating the activities of other Federal agencies and volunteer organizations.
- Managing the President's Disaster Relief Fund.

The Stafford Act established the Presidential Declaration Process. There are four steps in this process:

- Step 1. A joint FEMA/State Preliminary Damage Assessment (PDA)
- Step 2. The Governor's request for assistance
- Step 3. FEMA's recommendation to the President regarding the request
- Step 4. The Presidential declaration

When a disaster is considered "catastrophic," the sequence differs in that the PDA is conducted after the Presidential declaration. The declaration process is described in more detail in the next lesson.

Pre-Disaster Relations

Before disaster strikes, tribes should have emergency operations plans. Tribes also should be included in emergency management networks with local, State, and Federal partners.

However, many tribal governments currently lack emergency management resources and training. To help build emergency management capability:

- Tribal representatives can take emergency management courses, including a classroom course designed specifically for tribal governments to help them build emergency management capabilities.
- Staff in FEMA Regional Offices can work with tribes to develop emergency operations plans, encourage participation in programs such as the National Flood Insurance Program (NFIP), obtain flood insurance rate maps through the NFIP, and help tribes gain the funds and technical assistance needed to develop their ability to carry out emergency functions.

Preparing for Disaster

Tribal governments are prepared for disasters.

Tim Sanders, Emergency Manager, Gila River Indian Community

Tribal government does take their responsibility to their members very, very seriously. Our program at Gila River is set up so that we provide individual and family assistance on a routine basis for these emergency situations, so we'll actually fund repairs to homes, put people up in temporary housing and things like that. We take care of the individuals and families and we take care of the tribal infrastructure.

Lawrence Lucero, Elected Official, Isleta Pueblo

And I would hope that funding for planning would be made available and providing technical assistance to tribes so that the Federal Government, which is FEMA, could also fulfill that part of their trust responsibility to making sure that tribes are prepared for disasters in the event that they were to occur.

Tribal Status

A condition of Federal assistance is that a tribe must be federally recognized. The tribal status needs to be determined before initial contacts are made.

The Bureau of Indian Affairs (BIA) list recognized tribes, and updates the list regularly. Listed tribes are:

- Granted status as sovereign nations.
- Included in the U.S. Government Federal trust responsibility.

Federal Recognition

Over 500 tribes are recognized by the Federal Government. There are a few tribes that are recognized by States, but not by the Federal Government. Unlisted tribes petition the Bureau of Indian Affairs for Federal recognition. If recognition is granted, tribes receive sovereign government status, appear on the list of recognized tribes, and have a Federal trust relationship with the Federal Government. Federal recognition can happen only two ways: (1) recognition by an act of Congress, or (2) recognition by the Department of the Interior following a lengthy and complex recognition process undertaken by the tribe. This Federal acknowledgement process can average between 10 and 17 years.

Federal Trust Responsibility

The Federal Government has a trust responsibility to federally recognized Indian tribes that arises from Indian treaties, statutes, Executive orders, and the historical relations between the United States and Indian tribes. While the exact legal boundaries of the Federal trust responsibility have not been fully defined, the trust responsibility consists of general and specific components (although the line between these two components is not always clear).

The general component of the trust responsibility relates to the United States' unique legal and political relationship with federally recognized Indian tribes. It informs Federal policy and provides that the Federal Government consult with and consider the interests of the tribes when taking actions that may affect tribes or their resources. Courts have not required particular procedures, but generally have looked to see whether Federal agencies have sought the views of tribes and considered their interests. The general trust provides one basis for the legal principle that ambiguities or doubts in statutes must be construed in favor of Indians.

The specific component of the trust responsibility ordinarily arises only from a formal action of the United States such as a statute, treaty, or Executive order. The trust is a fiduciary relationship when Congress directs a Federal agency to manage resources such as timber or lands for the benefit of tribes.

Who Is Indian?

Tribes determine how to organize their governments and they also determine who is Indian. Do not assume someone is or is not an Indian based on appearance. An Indian is someone who:

- Has a quantum, or percentage, of Indian blood set by an individual tribe as the criterion for membership.
- Is recognized by that tribe as a member.

If you have Indian ancestry, remember that ancestry alone does not make you an Indian. Therefore, avoid reference to your Indian heritage when representing your agency at initial meetings with tribes.

Contacting Tribes

Any official relationship with a tribe begins with an introductory meeting with the tribe's elected leadership. To prepare for a meeting:

- Review information about the tribe. Tribal Web sites describe tribes and identify current leaders. Many tribes have publications that they are pleased to share upon request.

- Respect tribal protocol. Every tribe has a procedure for contacting and arranging meetings with tribal officials.
- Contact the FEMA Regional Tribal Liaison or others experienced in working with the tribes and ask for help arranging the meeting. These resources can help with questions about tribal protocol.

Tribal Decisionmaking

Elected tribal leaders make all significant decisions for tribes. Factors to remember when discussing issues or proposals with the leadership are:

- Respect for tribal sovereignty is the key to successful relations.
- Council resolutions are the means used to establish emergency management programs and authorize actions related to disaster assistance, hazard mitigation, and other programs.
- Tribal lawyers attend most council meetings, and can advise on resolutions and other legal matters.
- Meetings of tribal governing bodies proceed deliberately and address issues that may have higher priority to the tribe than emergency management or disaster matters.
- Tribes work on their own timetable. It is important for tribes to get to know you before doing business with you. This can result in the extension of normal deadlines.

Explaining Disaster Assistance

Tribes may need information about the declaration process, types of assistance available, and how to apply for assistance.

Many tribes view the Stafford Act requirement that State Governors request disaster assistance as a violation of tribal sovereignty. To respond to such concerns:

- Explain that as a Federal employee, you cannot go beyond the authority granted you by your agency and the law.
- Assure the tribal leadership that all programs and assistance will be delivered to the full extent possible, and that after there is a declaration, FEMA will communicate with the tribe on a government-to-government basis.

Advice to Tribes

Personal trust often develops between tribal, State, and Federal personnel as they work together during and after a disaster. This bond may lead to a lasting emergency management partnership, giving tribes access to mutual assistance agreements, communications links, and other benefits.

A good relationship is also important in ensuring that the State requests Federal declaration for the tribes when damage warrants such a request.

Tribal governments do have the option, once the declaration is approved, of applying for Public Assistance grants and the Hazard Mitigation Grant Program directly, as grantees. The Public Assistance and Hazard Mitigation lessons of this course describe factors that tribes need to consider to make informed decisions.

State Role in Disaster Assistance

The Stafford Act gives States control over disaster assistance funding, except when tribes choose to be grantees under the Public Assistance program or Hazard Mitigation Grant Program. Some States may not consider tribal communities eligible for disaster assistance. A State following such a policy should be informed that Indians are dual citizens of the tribe and the United States, and are entitled to the same services as every other citizen of the State. One condition of all Federal grant programs is an agreement to administer benefits to all eligible citizens. The equal protection clause of the 14th amendment to the U.S. Constitution also applies.

Setting Realistic Expectations

Tribal officials need to understand what disaster assistance can and cannot do. Be sure to make the following points when explaining disaster assistance:

- Disaster assistance is limited to repairing damage from this event only. Preexisting damage is not eligible.
- Facilities owned by other Federal agencies, such as the Bureau of Indian Affairs, will not be eligible for repair or replacement. An exception to this is that roads owned by the Bureau of Indian Affairs are eligible for disaster assistance.

Resources

- FEMA's Tribal Web site [https://www.fema.gov/fema-tribal-affairs]
- American Indian and Alaska Native Data and Links [http://factfinder.census.gov/home/aian/index.htm]
- Tribal Directory [http://www.bia.gov/WhoWeAre/BIA/OIS/TribalGovernmentServices/TribalDirectory/index.htm]
- Robert T. Stafford Disaster Relief and Emergency Assistance Act [https://www.fema.gov/robert-t-stafford-disaster-relief-and-emergency-assistance-act-public-law-93-288-amended]

Increase your knowledge by reading books and materials about Indian people and their culture. Suggestions:

1. Basso, Keith H. *Western Apache Language and Culture*. The University of Arizona Press, Tucson and London, 1990.
2. Beall, Merrill D. *I Will Fight No More Forever: Chief Joseph and the Nez Perce War*. University of Washington Press, 1963.
3. Brown, Dee. *Bury My Heart At Wounded Knee*. Holt, Reinhart and Winston, 1970.
4. Canby, William C. *American Indian Law in a Nutshell*. West Group, St. Paul, Minnesota, 1998.
5. Clifton, James A. *Being and Becoming Indian*. The Dorsey Press, Chicago, 1989.
6. Deloria, Vine, Jr. *Custer Died For Your Sins*. University of Oklahoma Press, Norman and London, 1969.
7. Diaz, Bernal. *The Conquest of Mexico: The Diary of Bernal Diaz*.
8. Dooling, D.M., and Paul Jordon-Smith (editors). *I Become Part of It: Sacred Dimensions in Native American Life*. Parabola Books, New York, 1989.
9. Eastman, Charles Alexander. *The Soul of an Indian*. The Classic Wisdom Collection, New World Library, San Rafael, California, 1993.
10. Erdoes, Richards, and Alfonso Ortiz (editors). *American Indian Myths and Legends*. Pantheon Books, New York, 1984.
11. Haines, Francis. *The Plains Indian*. Thomas Y. Crowell Company, New York, 1976.
12. Hanke, Lewis. *Aristotle and the American Indian*. Indian Press, 1970.
13. Highwater, Jamake. *Native Land: Sagas of North America*. Little, Brown and Company, Boston and Toronto, 1986.
14. Hultkrnatz, Ake. *Native Religions of North America*. Harper and Row, San Francisco, 1987.
15. Laubin, Reginald and Gladys. *The Indian Tipi: Its History, Construction and Use*. University of Oklahoma Press, 1989.
16. Lincoln, Kenneth. *The Good Red Road*. Harper and Row Publishers, San Francisco, 1987.
17. Neihardt, John G. *Black Elk Speaks*. University of Nebraska Press, Lincoln, 1959.
18. Neihardt, John G. *Twilight of the Sioux*. University of Nebraska Press, Lincoln, 1971.
19. Padden, R.C. *Hummingbird and the Hawk*.
20. Ross, A.C. *Mitakuye Oyasin: We Are All Related*. Bear Press, 1990.
21. Sale, Kirkpatrick. *The Conquest of Paradise*. Knoph Press, New York, 1990.
22. Stegner, Wallace. *Angle of Repose*. *Just good reading about the West.
23. Stegner, Wallace. *Where the Bluebird Sings to the Lemonade Springs*. *Just good reading about the West.
24. Weatherford, Jack. *Indian Givers: How the Indians Transformed the World*. Fawcett Columbine, New York, 1988.
25. Weatherford, Jack. *Native Roots: How the Indians Enriched America*. Fawcett Columbine, New York, 1991.
26. Wilkinson, Charles. *Blood Struggle: the Rise of Modern Indian Nations*. W.W. Norton & Co., New York, 2005.
27. Wolfson, Evelyn. *Growing Up Indian*. Walker and Company, New York, 1986.

*Young teen reading.

Lesson 5: Tribal Relations - Individual Assistance

Individual Assistance Programs

When the President declares a major disaster, a wide range of assistance becomes available to individual disaster victims. Individual Assistance programs meet a variety of individual needs, depending on the disaster.

The Robert T. Stafford Disaster Relief and Emergency Assistance Act (PL 93-288, as amended) specifies the order in which assistance should be provided. The delivery sequence is:

- Emergency assistance provided by voluntary agencies
- Insurance
- Individuals and Households Program (IHP) Housing Assistance
- Small Business Administration loans
- IHP Other Assistance
- Additional assistance
- The Cora Brown Fund

Emergency Assistance

Local agencies such as the fire department, emergency medical services, American Red Cross, and other voluntary agencies provide emergency assistance during immediate response. Emergency needs include:

- Shelter
- Food
- Clothing
- First aid

Insurance

Applicants pursue assistance through their private insurance carriers. If the insurance settlement is delayed, insurance is insufficient, or claims are denied, applicants may receive IHP Housing Assistance, but must guarantee repayment of FEMA funds if insurance covers the losses.

IHP Housing Assistance

The IHP provides Housing Assistance and Other Assistance either in the form of cash grants up to $25,000 per individual or household per disaster, or unlimited direct assistance.
IHP Housing Assistance is administered and funded by FEMA. Assistance may include the following:

- Temporary Housing
- Repair Assistance
- Replacement Assistance
- Permanent Housing Construction Assistance

Small Business Administration (SBA) Loans

Low-interest disaster loans are available for homeowners, renters, business owners, and nonprofit organizations. This program is administered and funded by the SBA under its own authority.

IHP Other Assistance Program

This program provides grants to meet disaster-related serious needs and necessary expenses not covered by other governmental assistance programs, insurance, or other means. IHP Other Assistance combined with all other assistance provided to an individual or household cannot exceed $25,000 for a single disaster.
IHP Other Assistance funds may be provided under the following categories:

- Medical, dental, and funeral expenses
- Personal property, transportation, moving and storage, and other expenses

FEMA funds 75 percent of the program grants, and the State funds 25 percent.

Other Individual Assistance Programs

Other Individual Assistance programs are:

- Disaster Unemployment Assistance (DUA)
- Crisis Counseling Assistance (CC)
- Disaster Legal Services (DLS)
- The Cora Brown Fund

Tribal Relations and Individual Assistance

The Individual Assistance staff faces challenges delivering programs to tribal governments. Challenges may include:

- Lack of familiarity of tribal leadership with FEMA's Individual Assistance programs.
- Isolation caused by distance, lack of telephones, and lack of transportation that hampers communication.
- Difficulty determining home ownership.
- The need for all disaster staff to know and observe tribal protocol and cultural issues.

Spreading FEMA's Message

A big challenge for Individual Assistance is getting FEMA's message to eligible tribal applicants. Possible explanations for this difficulty include the following:

- Tribal leaders may not be familiar with basic program information needed to lend their support to FEMA's efforts.
- Usual media outlets do not reach many in the community, who instead rely on tribal newspapers and radio stations.
- The area may be rural and require house-to-house contacts.

Tips for Spreading the Message

It is important that tribal leadership understand the benefits of programs offered by FEMA and others and how to access these programs. One way the leaders can use the information to support FEMA's efforts is by encouraging people impacted by the disaster to register and explaining what they need to do.

FEMA's list of media outlets usually does not include small, low-wattage tribal radio stations or tribal newspapers and newsletters, and these should be added to the list. Posters and fliers need to be placed at community centers, restaurants, or other locations where tribal members congregate. Individual Assistance staff can work with FEMA's External Affairs staff to identify and target tribal media and other communication channels.

Aiding Registration

Even after the message is spread throughout the community, the following factors may prevent some individuals from applying:

- Some people may not trust the Government and will not apply for assistance.
- People without access to telephones cannot call the National Processing Service Centers (NPSCs).
- Language barriers may prevent some from applying.
- The elderly may require special help.
- Multiple families may reside in the same dwelling and not realize that each family needs to file an application.

Registration Tips

FEMA depends on the National Processing Service Centers (NPSCs) to take most applications for assistance over the telephone and process these requests. According to a 1999 survey, only 39 percent of native households in rural communities have telephones. FEMA staff has used alternatives such as interviewing individuals and preparing applications on paper, or using cell phones to help people register.

Locating and registering all potentially eligible residents on a reservation may be impossible without help from the tribe. Often roads on reservations are not paved, and there are no addresses or mailboxes. Community Relations can partner with tribal representatives, or the tribal governing bodies may send tribal members with cell phones to locate and help these people register.

Also, a scheduled tribal social event such as a powwow typically brings most of the tribe to one location. Disaster workers can arrange to set up a registration booth at the event.

Registration Process

If someone calls to register who has suffered damage but there has been no declaration, the caller will be referred to the tribal emergency manager or tribal officials as well as voluntary agencies assisting with the event.

The callers may be asked the questions, "Are you under tribal jurisdiction?" or "Do you reside on tribal lands?" This is done to identify tribal applicants for coordination of FEMA inspections, avoid duplication of benefits, and determine the amount of assistance provided to various jurisdictions.

Applications submitted by non-Native Americans who live on tribal lands in the declared areas are processed the same as other applications.

Housing Ownership

On an Indian reservation, there are several types of housing arrangements and various responsibilities for repair and maintenance of properties.

Arrangement	**Responsibilities**
Individual Owns House, But Not Land	An individual may own the house but not the land. In such situations, the land may be owned by the tribe or held in trust by the Bureau of Indian Affairs (BIA), and either the land cannot be deeded, or if a deed can be issued, it will not be a traditional deed of trust.
Tribal Housing Authority Owns Housing	Tribal Housing Authorities, through grants from the Department of Housing and Urban Development (HUD), build new homes that individuals can purchase from the Authorities. The Authority, considered the owner until final payment is made, is responsible for maintenance and repair. The Authority may be able to apply through Public Assistance for funds to repair uninsured housing owned by the Authority.

BIA Owns Housing	BIA funds housing on reservations. Unless ownership is conveyed to the individual, repairs and maintenance of the housing are the responsibility of BIA.
Individual Is a Conventional Homeowner	Conventional homeowners paid outright or through mortgage lending agencies for their homes.
Individual Inherited Home	Homeowners inherited the home, and the title may or may not have been transferred.
Individual Rents Tribally Owned Housing	Traditional renters pay a fee or live rent-free in the dwelling.

Occupancy and Ownership on Reservations

The Native American Housing and Self-Determination Act allows for the establishment of private, nonprofit Tribal Housing Authorities. HUD funds construction of much tribal housing, but Tribal Housing Authorities usually own the housing. HUD funds are channeled to the Authorities through the Indian Comprehensive Development Block Grants (ICDBG) and Indian Housing Block Grants (IHBG). Residents make a series of regular payments and assume ownership after making a final payment. Residents who are homeowners may apply for housing repair assistance under the Individuals and Households Program. Those who have not made a final payment and do not hold title to the housing may be eligible for rental assistance.

Homeowners may assume that they applied for housing repair assistance under the Individual Assistance program because the Tribal Housing Authority viewed their damage. Comparing Tribal Housing Authority lists with FEMA registrations can help identify those who are the Authority's responsibility versus those who own their homes and may be eligible for assistance from FEMA. This list is also helpful in sorting out questions from housing inspectors concerning home ownership.

BIA Role

The BIA is often perceived to be the agency authorized to oversee all the activities on reservations. This perception is incorrect. The responsibility of the BIA is primarily the administration and management of land held in trust by the United States for the Indians and Indian tribes. On some reservations, the BIA along with Indian Health Services provides health and human services similar to services that States and county governments provide to their constituents. Depending on the relationship with the tribe, the BIA Superintendent may be a good source to contact about protocols on the reservation, people who should be involved with a particular program, and the status of tribal lands.

Preparing To Inspect Housing

Tribal governments should be asked how they want housing inspections conducted. Points to cover include:

- The protocol that inspectors should follow to get permission to enter tribal lands.
- Whether a tribe would like representatives to accompany inspectors.

Protocols will vary based on the tribe. Where possible, these should be worked out before an event occurs.

Briefing Inspectors

After determining the tribes' preferences on conducting inspections, Individual Assistance staff should inform the housing inspectors about tribal protocols early in the process, during contract briefings. Problems can be avoided or reduced if:

- Inspectors know the requirements from the outset.
- All inspectors receive consistent information.

A Tribal Housing Authority representative or other designated tribal representative should be contacted to help resolve questions about home ownership and obtain needed documentation.

Assistance From FEMA

The different amounts of grant assistance available from FEMA to repair housing can be an issue. For example:

- Public Assistance (PA) funds can be used to restore tribally owned, uninsured housing to pre-disaster conditions.
- Individual Assistance (IA) funds are limited to making individually owned housing safe, sanitary, and fit to occupy.

Explaining the cost-share requirement with PA funds will help reduce concerns about inequities.

Renters

Renters reside in housing owned by someone else for which they pay rent or live rent-free. Individuals may be eligible for funds (based on fair market rates) under the Individuals and Households Program to pay for similar alternate housing if their residence is determined to be nonfunctional.

Homeowners

Residents who are homeowners may apply for housing repair assistance under the Individuals and Households Program. The amount of assistance is limited to restoring the home to a safe and sanitary living or functioning condition. Cosmetic repair, such as replacement of stained siding or carpeting, is not eligible. Homeowners need to find their own contractors and monitor the repair process. Unscrupulous contractors are a persistent problem. Try to work through the tribe, and let them recommend contractors.

Occupants of Tribally Owned Housing

The Tribal Housing Authority should be informed immediately to apply for Public Assistance, if the disaster declaration includes PA, for assistance to make housing repairs and to follow all requirements to document expenses for the program. Undocumented expenses cannot be reimbursed under Public Assistance.

Coordinating To Find Optimum Solutions

Many Indian reservations have a waiting list for housing and/or have a number of housing units in poor condition. Whether repairing disaster-damaged housing through the voluntary agencies, FEMA programs, Small Business Administration, or other Federal agencies, program staffs need to coordinate to direct funds toward optimum solutions for the individual occupants and for the tribe as a whole. Other Federal agencies include HUD and the BIA.

Replacement Housing

Mobile homes provide only temporary or short-term solutions, and disagreements over ownership and occupancy have caused problems on reservations. HUD funding may be available to build permanent replacement housing. The BIA has a Housing Improvement Program for lower income families and senior citizens, although funds are limited. Also, the Disaster Mitigation Act of 2000 allows FEMA to fund Permanent Housing Construction in remote areas where other types of housing cannot be used.

Matching Funds/Funding Packages

Public Assistance grants require matching funds, usually 25 percent. The Public Assistance program accepts in-kind matches of donated labor and materials. Under HUD's Community Development Block Grant (CDBG) program, funds lose their Federal identity and can be used for matching funds. For tribal grants, there must be reference made to their specific authority statute to verify if they may or may not be used to match other Federal grant programs.

Other Individual Assistance Programs

The tribe's relationship with the State affects delivery of Individual Assistance programs that require State involvement. These issues may include:

- Some States do not or cannot legally pay the Other Needs Assistance cost-share for tribal applicants.
- The State's mental health agency, which delivers the Crisis Counseling program, probably does not serve tribal governments.

Other Needs Assistance

Other Needs Assistance provides grants for personal property and transportation losses to homeowners, renters, and tenants of Tribal Housing Authority housing for those tribal members who cannot get an SBA loan. Other Needs Assistance requires a 25 percent State cost-share. Some States have laws that prohibit giving State funding to reservations. These States have to get the matching funds for Other Needs Assistance from the tribal governments. Other States have no legal prohibition, but may refuse to provide matching funds as a matter of policy.

Crisis Counseling

The State mental health delivery system usually does not include responsibility on Indian reservations, which traditionally do not receive State services. Tribal social service agencies could be possible recipients of Crisis Counseling funding to assure delivery of crisis counseling on reservations.

Resources

- Individual Assistance information on the FEMA Web site. [https://www.fema.gov/individual-assistance-program-tools]
- DisasterAssistance.gov provides information on disaster assistance from the U.S. Government before, during and after a disaster. [http://www.disasterassistance.gov]

Lesson 6: Tribal Relations - Public Assistance

Public Assistance

Public Assistance is supplementary assistance to local, State, and tribal governments and certain private nonprofit organizations for response and recovery in a major disaster or emergency.

One of the ways this assistance is provided is through Federal grants to help rebuild public facilities such as roads, bridges, buildings, utilities, and recreational facilities damaged by disasters.

FEMA funds a minimum of 75 percent of Public Assistance grants, and the grantee funds the balance. Tribal governments may receive Public Assistance grant funds as subgrantees of the State or directly as grantees.

Intent of Public Assistance

- To provide assistance to address immediate threats to life, public health, and safety; and to protect improved public and private properties.
- To ensure the public is served in a timely and efficient manner.
- To provide assistance to repair, restore, or replace eligible permanent facilities.
- To encourage mitigation measures.

Public Assistance Process

The Public Assistance (PA) process includes the following components:

- **Applicants' Briefing:** State emergency officials conduct a briefing to inform potential applicants of available assistance and the procedures for applying. The State is responsible for conducting one or more Applicants' Briefings.
- **Request for Public Assistance:** Applicants complete a Request for Public Assistance form to document their intention to apply for Public Assistance through the Public Assistance program.
- **Kickoff Meetings:** An applicant, the State, and FEMA meet to explain the PA process and procedures, discuss applicant damages, assess applicant needs, and explain eligibility. The participants then agree upon a plan of action. Kickoff Meetings ensure that applicants have the information needed to identify and complete a Public Assistance project. The State receives specific details on documentation and reporting requirements.
- **Project Formulation:** PA staff members work with applicants to complete documentation of proposed projects to ensure that projects meet Public Assistance eligibility criteria.
- **Project Worksheets:** PA staff members work with applicants as needed to complete Project Worksheets that provide FEMA with a detailed scope of work and an accurate cost estimate for each project.

Applicants are responsible for completing recovery actions, and are accountable for the use of Public Assistance grant funds.

Tribal Relations and Public Assistance

The Public Assistance staff must be ready to deal with likely issues in delivering the program to tribal governments. Possible issues are:

- Tribes may be left out of the Public Assistance communications loop.
- Missing and inaccurate damage estimates can prevent or delay program delivery.
- Identifying facilities ownership will require effort.
- Some tribes may need a thorough explanation of program requirements.

Tribal Participation

Eligible tribal applicants may need help starting the Public Assistance process. Public Assistance staff members should:

- Clarify State, Bureau Indian Affairs (BIA), and other Federal agency roles in addressing tribal damage to assure that tribes are included in the process.
- Involve the State. It is a good opportunity to foster Federal, tribal, and State partnerships.
- Observe tribal protocol when meeting with representatives. Meet first with the Tribal Chairman, or designee, who will generally direct you to the appropriate department heads.
- Avoid promising assistance beyond program limits.

Including Tribes in Preliminary Damage Assessments (PDAs) and Applicants' Briefings

A good tribal-State relationship smoothes program delivery. However, without day-to-day emergency management connections with tribes, States may overlook damage on affected tribal lands and potential tribal eligibility for Public Assistance. During PDA planning, FEMA needs to advocate assessment of tribal damages. The Regional staff should ensure that the PDA team includes tribal representatives, and that damages on tribal lands are included in PDA figures for Public Assistance.

PDA information on tribal damages will be used to determine the magnitude of the event, verify the need for supplemental assistance, identify immediate needs, and identify initial staffing and technical requirements. In addition, good PDA information will identify the proportion of State and/or tribal share of program costs.

If the tribe chooses to be a grantee, the tribe may request that FEMA staff conduct the Applicants' Briefing. If the tribe chooses to be a subgrantee, FEMA staff should check with States to ensure that the tribes participate in Applicants' Briefings. The tribe may participate in the Applicants' Briefing conducted for local officials or may prefer a separate tribal Applicants' Briefing. It may be necessary to make several contacts with the tribes to ensure that the right people know about the briefings and that the appropriate individuals attend.

Explaining the Public Assistance Program

It is a good idea to get to know tribal officials before disaster strikes and to let them know about the program. It may be necessary in the event of a disaster to revisit information about the types of assistance available and how to apply for this assistance. Know and observe tribal protocol when arranging an informational meeting. The FEMA Tribal Liaison is a good source of information for identifying the protocol for a particular tribe. Request the tribal public works manager and others who are responsible for the infrastructure attend the meeting. Be aware that during times of disaster, tribal representative are most likely working long and difficult hours, and may be exhausted.

Remember to avoid using terms such as "you should" and "you ought to." Better approaches are: "The types of assistance available through FEMA's Public Assistance program for which you may be eligible are…" or "This is how we can partner with you to meet your needs." Be careful to explain program limits, project accounting, and cost-share requirements, and be very clear about what the Public Assistance program can and cannot deliver.

Bureau of Indian Affairs (BIA) Role

The BIA can support tribal participation in the Public Assistance program by:

- Providing FEMA-trained inspectors to serve on PDA teams.
- Identifying BIA roads, schools, hospitals, and other public facilities.

Preliminary Damage Assessments (PDAs)

FEMA's Regional Office Tribal Liaison or Headquarters Tribal Liaison can contact the BIA to request services of the FEMA-trained BIA inspectors. The team will help conduct PDAs on tribal lands on very short notice. Inclusion in PDA totals puts tribes on track for involvement when the Public Assistance program begins. PDA documentation may provide a basis for developing damage estimates for Public Assistance projects.

Facilities Ownership

If possible, meet with the BIA prior to disaster events to establish a relationship and explain how they can be of service in the event of a Federal disaster. The BIA is responsible for some roads, schools, hospitals, and other public facilities on Indian reservations. Knowing ownership helps FEMA avoid paying for repairs that are the responsibility of another Federal agency.

The BIA can help identify the patchwork of other agencies that share responsibility for roads. A reservation may include Federal highways, county highways, BIA roads, and tribal roads. Federal highway funds are passed through the BIA to make repairs. The permanent restoration of disaster damage to county and tribally owned roads is eligible for Public Assistance funding.

Applicants' Briefing

Tribal Applicants' Briefings usually present more detail than standard presentations. When planning for or assisting with a briefing for a tribal community:

- Determine past disaster experience. Tribes without prior program experience may have more extensive information needs.
- Be prepared to explain questions about eligibility, floodplain management, insurance requirements, environmental and historic considerations, and Federal procurement standards.
- Plan to explain the differences between grantee and subgrantee status and the advantages and disadvantages of each.

Kickoff Meeting

Bring experienced staff members who can work with tribal representatives to explain:

- Program requirements and processes.
- Eligibility requirements.
- Documentation needed for reimbursement.
- Floodplain management considerations, insurance requirements, hazard mitigation opportunities, and compliance with environmental and historic preservation laws.

Providing sample forms that demonstrate what is required can help ensure desired outcomes.

Eligible Projects

If possible, Public Assistance staff should determine which damaged facilities are tribally owned and therefore eligible as Public Assistance projects before the Kickoff Meeting. Tribal officials, BIA, and other Federal representatives will be able to help resolve questions about ownership and responsibilities for tribal property.

Staffing the Kickoff Meeting

Some FEMA Disaster Assistance Employees are experienced at surveying disaster damage on Indian reservations. These employees work as Public Assistance Coordinators and Project Officers who help tribal representatives throughout the Public Assistance process. Contact the Tribal Liaison in the FEMA Region or at FEMA Headquarters to request the services of a specialized team.

Developing Project Worksheets

FEMA staff should plan to work closely with tribal representatives to develop Project Worksheets. Tribes usually provide space for the teams to work.

Grantee Versus Subgrantee Status

Federally recognized tribes may apply as grantees or subgrantees under the Public Assistance program. Some factors to consider are:

- A tribe may choose either status for current and future disasters.
- As grantees, tribes need to sign a FEMA/tribe agreement, develop a Public Assistance Administrative Plan, comply with audit requirements, and pay the required non-Federal share.
- As subgrantees, tribes often receive a portion of the non-Federal share from the State, but do not receive the grantee administrative allowance.

Grantee Status: Decision Factors

Financial concerns play a major role in a tribe's decision. Grantee responsibility for the non-Federal share is a requirement that FEMA staff needs to make clear. Tribes have raised the issue that the Federal Government should assume tribal cost-shares as part of its trust responsibility, and this issue is the subject of a current legal case. Tribes may also ask their congressional representatives to sponsor bills forgiving debts for matching funds. Regardless, FEMA staff must proceed with the 25 percent cost-share requirement, unless directed otherwise through judicial or legislative decisions.

Grantee status serves to recognize tribal sovereignty, always an important consideration for tribes. A tribe that chooses grantee status probably will need assistance to develop a Public Assistance Administrative Plan and to fulfill grant management responsibilities.

Subgrantee Status: Decision Factors

States already have staff trained to administer grants, saving tribes administrative time and expense. Also, most States provide a portion of the Public Assistance cost-share to subgrantees. Subgrantee status tends to strengthen the emergency management partnership between the tribe and the State. After weighing the cost and workload requirements, most tribes choose to apply as subgrantees.

Grant Management Issues

All Public Assistant applicants must maintain proper documentation. Audits show that tribes, like other applicants, often have problems documenting how work is done and recording the associated costs. To prevent problems, Public Assistance staff members should:

- Encourage tribes to participate in training available through FEMA to help them administer the program.
- Explain that failure to keep proper records can result in no funding or recovery of funds by FEMA.
- Provide extra help and monitoring as projects begin. Early support will pay off with fewer grant management problems.

Documenting Emergency Work

Take the opportunity at informational meetings and briefings to emphasize the importance of documenting expenses incurred when responding to any emergency. Personnel, equipment costs, and other expenses of the response should be tracked. Standardized forms for documenting costs can be distributed at meetings, and also are available on FEMA's Web site. If the event is declared, the tribe may be eligible for reimbursement of expenses. If the event is not declared, the information remains useful for emergency management purposes.

Example of Monitoring Help

A project by a tribal subgrantee required hiring a foreman and crew to do specialized work. FEMA and the State worked with the tribe to begin documenting the work using standard forms and procedures. Monitoring of recordkeeping continued as the work progressed.

Environmental/Historic Preservation Concerns

Public Assistance projects, whether located on or off Indian reservations, may raise environmental and historic preservation concerns.

Public Assistance staff should work with tribes to identify whether a project may affect the environment on tribal lands, disturb tribal historic or sacred sites, or reveal artifacts.

Tribes generally have designated representatives to assist with environmental and historic matters.

Environmental Requirements

The following statutes and Executive orders set environmental requirements:

- Clean Air Act
- Clean Water Act
- Coastal Zone Management Act
- Coastal Barrier Resources Act
- Resource Conservation & Recovery Act
- Endangered Species Act
- National Historic Preservation Act
- National Environmental Policy Act
- Executive Orders:
- Wetlands
- Floodplains
- Environmental Justice
- Protection of Children

Legal Responsibilities for Historic Preservation

FEMA must follow requirements set by the following statutes and Executive orders:

- National Historic Preservation Act
- Executive Order: Indian Sacred Sites
- American Indian Religious Freedom Act
- Native American Graves Protection and Repatriation Act

Historic properties that are most likely to involve Indian tribes include traditional cultural properties with religious and cultural significance and archeological sites.

Resources

- Public Assistance Grant Program [https://www.fema.gov/public-assistance-local-state-tribal-and-non-profit]
- Public Assistance Roles and Responsibilities [https://www.fema.gov/public-assistance-grant-application-process]
- Public Assistance Policy and Guidance [https://www.fema.gov/public-assistance-policy-and-guidance]
- Environmental Planning and Historic Preservation (EHP) Program [https://www.fema.gov/environmental-planning-and-historic-preservation-program]
- Principal Environmental & Historic Preservation Laws [https://www.fema.gov/environmental-planning-and-historic-preservation-program/principal-environmental-historic]
- Historic Preservation Information [http://www.fema.gov/environmental-planning-and-historic-preservation-program/historic-preservation-information]

Lesson 7: Tribal Relations - Hazard Mitigation

Mitigation Programs

What Is Mitigation?

Mitigation is any action of a long-term, permanent nature that reduces or eliminates the actual or potential risk of loss of life or property from a hazardous event.

FEMA encourages individuals, communities, States, tribal governments, and others to take preventive measures now rather than after an event. The Disaster Mitigation Act of 2000 requires all States, tribal governments, and local governments to meet mitigation planning requirements to receive mitigation project grants. Hazard identification and risk assessment information developed during the planning process serves as a guide for the mitigation measures that would be most beneficial and cost effective for individuals and the community.

Sample Mitigation Measures

Sample mitigation measures include:

- Acquisition of structures - Acquisition often is referred to as "buyouts." After acquired structures are demolished, property is devoted to open space.
- Relocation of structures - Relocation moves structures out of hazardous locations.
- Strengthening/retrofitting structures to withstand forces - Foundations, floors, walls, and roofs can be strengthened/retrofitted to prevent seismic or wind damage.
- Making utilities, structural components, and contents resistant to damage - Examples: Utilities such as water heaters can be strapped to prevent toppling in an earthquake, or they can be moved to a higher spot to prevent flood damage; shutters can protect windows from wind damage.
- Diverting the hazard - Structural means such as dikes or floodwalls built to divert hazards are often the most difficult and expensive to achieve.
- Elevating structures - Building the structure on stilts can prevent water damage from rising floodwaters or coastal waters.

Pre-Disaster Mitigation Programs/Activities

Pre-disaster mitigation focuses on mitigation planning, policies, actions, and projects aimed at preventing future damage.

- **National Flood Insurance Program (NFIP)**
  The NFIP makes federally backed flood insurance available in more than 19,000 communities. Communities must agree to adopt and enforce floodplain management ordinances to reduce future flood damage and to make that insurance available to their

community. Federally backed flood insurance is not available if a community does not join the NFIP. Hazard identification and floodplain mapping also are available through NFIP participation.

- **Increased Cost of Compliance (ICC)**
  The Increased Cost of Compliance program provides added coverage to standard flood insurance policies to supplement the cost of complying with State or community floodplain management laws.

- **Pre-Disaster Mitigation (PDM) Grants**
  FEMA awards competitive PDM grants for pre-disaster mitigation planning and projects that primarily address natural hazards. Implementation of projects identified in the plans reduces overall risks to the population and structures, while also reducing reliance on funding from federally declared disasters.

- **Flood Mitigation Assistance (FMA)**
  The Flood Mitigation Assistance program provides pre-disaster grants for both planning and implementation. Grant funds are made available from NFIP insurance premiums and are only available to communities participating in the NFIP.

Post-Disaster Mitigation: Hazard Mitigation Grant Program (HMGP)

After a disaster declaration, the Hazard Mitigation Grant Program funds mitigation projects that substantially reduce the risk of future damages.

HMGP objectives include:

- To identify and implement cost-effective mitigation measures that will reduce future losses.
- To coordinate mitigation needs with existing State and Federal efforts.
- To capitalize upon previous mitigation planning efforts to maximize the financial opportunities available under the HMGP.

The amount of funding is based on Federal expenditures during the disaster response and recovery.

Tribal Relations and Mitigation

Mitigation poses challenges to tribal governments. Tribes must:

- Invest time and effort to meet planning requirements for mitigation.
- Weigh the advantages and disadvantages of grantee and subgrantee status under the HMGP. In some cases it is illegal for the State to represent the tribe.

- Overcome barriers to NFIP participation by getting tribal lands mapped and passing floodplain ordinances.

Building Mitigation Partnerships

In working with tribes to promote mitigation:

- Provide careful explanations of mitigation and NFIP programs and requirements.
- Offer to meet with tribal leaders and the tribal council to explain planning and NFIP requirements.
- If the tribe is to act as subgrantee, offer to provide assistance to the tribe to develop a project that will meet HMGP eligibility requirements.
- Suggest ways to gain the greatest benefit from available funding.
- Find partners within the tribal administration, such as Water Resources or Emergency Management agencies, to bring proposals to the tribal council.

Explaining Mitigation Programs

Tribes may be eligible for HMGP funding after a declared disaster. If the tribe is a subgrantee of the State, partnership with the State is important to ensure that potential tribal projects are identified and included for eligibility review. The State accepts and prioritizes the projects for eligibility review. If the tribal project is selected, the project is submitted by the State to FEMA for eligibility review and approval. If the tribe is the grantee, the amount of damage on tribal lands determines the amount of HMGP funds available. Projects will go directly to FEMA from the tribal government.

Mitigation programs such as Flood Mitigation Assistance and Pre-Disaster Mitigation offer nondisaster funding for mitigation projects.

NFIP participation can provide tribes with improved insurance coverage and an incentive for developers.

Leveraging Funding

Matching funds for mitigation grants can come from a variety of sources.

In-kind contributions of goods and services are allowed as partial matches for most mitigation programs. The tribal government's expenditure of goods and services may be considered part of the cash match under FMA.

Federal funds from Department of Housing and Urban Development Community Development Block Grants (CDBG) and those awarded for self-determination contracts by the Bureau of Indian Affairs and Indian Health Services can potentially be used to meet matching or cost participation requirements. Refer to the specific authority statute to verify whether funds can match other Federal grant programs and check with the contracting officer.

Loan funds from the U.S. Small Business Administration and Farmer's Home Administration lose their Federal identity once the loan to the individual is approved. Therefore, homeowners can supply funds from either of these sources to match mitigation grant funds.

Increased Cost of Compliance coverage benefits under the National Flood Insurance Program may be used for elevation and/or acquisition location costs.

HMGP Applicants' Briefings

The State generally conducts Applicants' Briefings unless the tribe plans to be the grantee, in which case FEMA would conduct the briefing. If the State is responsible for the briefing, tribal representatives can attend the same briefings as local communities or they can request that a separate briefing be held for the tribe. Staff should assure that the briefings:

- Serve to form or strengthen mitigation partnerships with a tribe.
- Include HMGP steps and timelines, and aids such as sample mitigation plans and project applications.
- Explain differences between grantee and subgrantee status.

Mitigation Planning

To receive PDM, HMGP, and other mitigation grant funds, tribes need to develop mitigation plans. Mitigation personnel should:

- Describe planning as avoiding damage rather than preparing for disasters. According to grassroots sentiment, if you prepare, it will happen.
- Provide technical assistance. Most tribes probably need help developing required mitigation plans. Tribes choosing grantee status under the HMGP will especially need help meeting planning requirements as well as administering the program.

Building Tribal Planning Capability

Tribes do not receive tax revenue to pay for staffing, and need to be resourceful to do mitigation planning with limited funds.

The Environmental Protection Agency (EPA) will pay for some staff time to do all-hazards planning. The FMA program provides grants for planning.

PDM funding has been made available to tribes through the States. Tribes also can compete for planning funds through the PDM competitive grant program. Both PDM grants require up to a 25% match from tribes.

Grantee Versus Subgrantee Status

Tribes may apply as grantees or subgrantees under the HMGP and/or the Public Assistance (PA) program. Some factors to consider include the following:

- A tribe may choose either status for current and future disasters, and may choose a different status for the HMGP and the PA program for the same disaster.
- As grantees, tribes need to develop a mitigation plan and pay the entire grant cost-share.
- As subgrantees, tribes may not have to pay the full 25% match, as some States will pay a percentage of the cost-share.

Grantee Status: Decision Factors

Financial concerns play a major role in a tribe's decision. Some State laws forbid giving State funds to Indian reservations, so the tribe must pay the entire grant cost-share. Other States do not provide any of the cost-share as a policy decision.

Grantee responsibility for cost-share is a requirement that FEMA staff needs to make clear. Tribes have raised the issue that the Federal Government should assume tribal cost-shares as part of their trust responsibility, and this issue is the subject of a current legal case. Tribes may also ask their congressional representatives to sponsor bills forgiving debts for matching funds. Regardless, FEMA staff must proceed with the 25% cost-share requirement, unless directed otherwise through judicial or legislative decisions.

Grantee status serves to recognize tribal sovereignty, always an important consideration for tribes. Many tribes lack the mitigation plans and planning staff needed to be grantees, but are interested in boosting their mitigation capability.

A tribe that chooses grantee status probably will need assistance to develop a mitigation plan and to fulfill grant management responsibilities.

Subgrantee Status: Decision Factors

States already have staff trained to administer grants, saving tribes administrative time and expense. Also, most States provide a portion of the HMGP cost-share to subgrantees. Subgrantee status tends to strengthen the emergency management partnership between the tribe and the State. After weighing the alternatives, most tribes choose to apply as subgrantees. Additionally, the tribe may have the ability to apply for more money as the subgrantee.

Reasons To Join the National Flood Insurance Program

Tribal governments show increasing interest in NFIP participation. These communities may want to participate in the NFIP because:

- Floodplain mapping allows planning, so people can be moved out of harm's way.
- The NFIP offers comprehensive insurance coverage that does not follow claims with fee increases or dropped policies.
- Potential developers want to insure projects on reservations, but insurance is not available without floodplain management.
- Tribes gain control over State and Federal construction projects that would alter water flows.

Insuring Tribal Buildings

Tribes benefit by buying insurance coverage for the repair and replacement of buildings as well as contents.

NFIP and Economic Development

Venture capital groups may be interested in developing projects such as mini-malls, casinos, hospitals, marinas, and golf courses on reservations, and need to know if proposed development is in a floodplain. Also, if land is earmarked for recreational development, floodplain ordinances can be used to prevent building residential structures.

Control Over Water Flows

With a floodplain ordinance in place, local, State, and Federal construction projects on or near a reservation require permits from the tribe, and cannot alter water flow on tribal lands.

NFIP Adoption Process

Advice and information should be provided to tribes throughout the adoption process. Below is a list of steps that tribes follow to participate in the NFIP:

- First, a tribal agency will review information about the NFIP to decide whether the tribe should join.
- After deciding to recommend NFIP membership, the agency will present a model resolution to the tribal council stating the tribe's intention to participate.
- Tribes should then work with FEMA to decide what should be studied.
- Following passage of the resolution, the council may need support to adopt or develop a floodplain ordinance.
- Finally, flood maps will be developed as funding becomes available.

Tribal NFIP Sponsor

To introduce the NFIP to a tribe, first establish a relationship with a local agency within the tribal government such as Emergency Management or Water Resources. The agency staff can discuss reasons to join or not join the NFIP.

Tribal Resolution To Join the NFIP

If the agency manager is convinced that the tribe should join, he or she can sponsor a resolution in writing from the tribal council stating the tribe's intention to participate in the NFIP. The resolution should establish organizational control for floodplain management.

Floodplain Ordinance

Next, the tribe needs to pass a floodplain ordinance. Tribes can choose whether to follow the State's ordinance or to create their own. FEMA can supply a sample ordinance for tribes to give to their attorneys and put in their own format without changing the content.

Resources

- How To Guide #1 "Getting Started: Building Support For Mitigation Planning" [http://www.fema.gov/library/viewRecord.do?id=1867]
- How To Guide #2 "Understanding Your Community's Risks, Identifying Hazards, and Determining Risks" [http://www.fema.gov/library/viewRecord.do?id=1880]
- How To Guide #7 "Integrating Human Caused Hazards into Mitigation Planning" [http://www.fema.gov/library/viewRecord.do?id=1915]

The following Web sites provide more information about mitigation programs:

- Mitigation Information [https://www.fema.gov/what-mitigation]
- Mitigation Best Practices Portfolio [https://www.fema.gov/what-mitigation#8]
- The National Flood Insurance Program [https://www.fema.gov/national-flood-insurance-program]
- Hazard Information [https://www.fema.gov/hazard-mitigation-assistance]
- Preparing for Disaster for People with Disabilities and other Special Needs [http://www.fema.gov/library/viewRecord.do?id=1442]
- FEMA's Tribal Multi-Hazard Mitigation Planning Guidance. [https://www.fema.gov/media-library/assets/documents/18355]

www.ingramcontent.com/pod-product-compliance
Lightning Source LLC
Chambersburg PA
CBHW080816280726
48660CB00018B/3469